ALL VIENNA

Text, photographs, lay-out and reproduction, entirely designed and created by the Technical Department of EDITORIAL ESCUDO DE ORO, S.A.

Rights of total or partial reproduction and translation reserved.

1st Edition, March 1981

I.S.B.N. 84-378-0268-7

Spanish	84-378-0788-3
French	84-378-0789-1
English	84-378-0790-5
German	84-378-0791-3
Italian	84-378-0792-1
Dutch	84-378-0793-X

Dep. Legal B. 4445-XXIV

GENERAL DISTRIBUTOR FOR AUSTRIA: RAU COLOR
1030 Wien, Weissgerberlände 56 und 60
Tel. 73 13 83

Impreso en España - Printed in Spain
F.I.S.A. Palaudarias, 26 - Barcelona-4

"Viena: view from the Belvedere." Painting by Bernardo Bellotto.

ANCIENT, IMPERIAL VIENNA

As a result of its exceptional geographic position — located between the Danube and the Alps, which slope gently down towards the hills called Wienerwald, the Woods of Vienna — the capital of Austria has been a fundamentally important factor for Europe throughout the city's dynamic, glorious history. Because it stands at the crossroads of the great routes of West and East Europe, Vienna soon became the heart of the continent.

The present-day federal capital — which is at the same time one of the nine states of the Federal State of Austria — not only constitutes a communications link with the Alpine region, but is also the centre of the Danube area. In their efforts to defend the Mediterranean and their territories against invasion from the north, the Romans — under the Emperor Augustus — occupied the area from the Eastern Alps to the Danube. Under the Emperor Tiberius, the 15th Legion established the oldest — and strongest — military camp in Austria, CARNUNTUM, which was the region's capital for almost 400 years. The frontier entrenchment of Limes was constructed around the year 50 AD, in the time of the Emperor Claudius. A camp for auxiliary Roman troops, Vindobona, was established in what is now the third district of Vienna, as a lateral defence for the stronghold of Carnuntum. Around 115 AD, when Trajan was emperor, the main part of the army was definitively transferred to Vin-

dobona. A difficult period ensued, and in the year 400 Vindobona was devastated by the passage of the Visigoths.

Not until Otto the Great re-established the Eastern March, around 960, did the country live in relative peace again. The word "Ostarichi" (Austrians) was first mentioned towards the end of the 10th century, in a document signed by Otto III: this is, as it were, the birth certificate of historical Austria. In 1137 Vienna was designated for the first time as a city. In the Regensburg imperial diet of 1156 the Eastern March was raised to the status of a duchy and Vienna (then called Vienni) was appointed its capital. The origin of the name Vienni is unknown, as is also the case with Vindomina and Vindobona, the city's former names. At this time a series of sovereigns — Duke Rudolf, Duke Heinrich Jasomirgott, Duke Leopold the Glorious — laid the foundations of Vienna as we see it today.

When Duke Friedrich II fell in a battle with the Hungarians, in 1246, the House of Babenberg, which had governed the history of Vienna for more than 300 years, ceased to exist. After the Battle of Dürnkrut, in the late 13th century, between Rudolf I of Hapsburg and Ottokar Przemysl, the king of Bohemia, the Hapsburg dynasty became closely linked with the history of Vienna and of all Austria.

The decision taken by the Emperor Ferdinand I in 1521, to transfer to Vienna the residence of the emperor of the Holy Roman-Germanic Empire, was of enormous historical importance. In 1529 and 1683 the walled city of Vienna successfully resisted siege by Turkish troops. Above all, the inhabitants' victory in 1683 saved Europe and prevented the destruction of Western civilization.

By virtue of its special characteristics, as a state embracing more than one nation, Vienna became a crucible of the cultures of East and West. In the 18th

S Stephen's Cathedral: details of the pulpit.

century, when the Baroque style revolutionized its architectural appearance, Vienna was considered the most beautiful city: ''glorious Vienna.'' In that century — which marks a vital landmark in Vienna's development — new buildings were raised, including the elegant Schönbrunn and Belvedere palaces for the nobility, and also S Charles' Church and the famous Gala Room of the National Library.

After Austria's declaration of war on Napoleon in 1813 and the signature of the Quadruple Alliance with Bavaria, Prussia and Russia, Vienna became the historic seat of the Congress bearing its name, in the course of which Prince Metternich played an important part in the distribution of modern Europe.

The city walls were demolished in the mid-19th century, when Franz Josef I was Emperor, so as to facilitate the modern city's expansion. This is when the Ring came into being: one of the most impressive, beautiful boulevards in the world, flanked by fine gardens and sumptuous monuments. A whole range of architectural styles is represented here; today the Ring Avenue constitutes one of the most fascinating promenades in Europe. The capital of Austria underwent great expansion in the second half of last century. The modern city sprang up — in contrast with the ancient city, and with baroque Vienna — at the end of the 19th century, under the auspices of Modernism (Jugendstil). Nowadays the different areas, with their wealth of monuments, make up an impressive ensemble.

The Emperor Franz Josef I died during the first World War and the Hapsburg dynasty was extinguished with him. The first Republic was proclaimed in 1918, and in 1938 Austria was annexed by Hitler's Germany. Ten years were to elapse after its liberation in 1945 before Vienna once again became the capital of Austria as a free country.

S Stephen's Cathedral: interior.

S Stephen's Cathedral: detail of the pulpit; the Virgin of Mercy or "Virgin of the Protecting Mantle."

The high altar in S Stephen's Cathedral. ▷

S STEPHEN'S CATHEDRAL

S Stephen's Cathedral, located in the original nucleus of the city, at the south-east corner of the old Roman fort, marks the geographical centre of Vienna, well-known all over the world. The plans that were to give the cathedral the essential part of its present-day appearance were drawn up by an unknown architect with the patronage of Duke Rudolf IV, its founder. The foundation stone of the nave, in the flamboyant Gothic style, was laid in 1359; the south tower was begun around 1365 and finished, by Hans von Prachatitz, in 1433; whereas the centre section was not concluded (by Hans Puchsbaum) until 1455. This architect began to build the north tower in 1467, but only the lower half was completed; from 1511 onwards there was no significant work on it. From 1556 to 1570 a Renaissance cupola was added to the unfinished tower. The Gothic bell-tower, 137 metres high, is the distinguishing feature of Vienna, for its graceful silhouette is visible against the sky from all over the city. Entrance to the church is via the Romanesque doorway, which is surmounted by the two Towers of the Pagans, 64 metres high. From the cathedral's nave one can view the church, divided into three parts by means of twelve columns. The grandeur and harmony of this Gothic building are impressive, colossal. In the left nave-aisle, above the large retable of the "Altar of New Citizens of Vienna" (Wiener Neustädteraltar), the visitor will see the initials A.E.I.O.U. in a masterly wood carving. These letters correspond to Frederick III's motto; his tomb is in the right nave-aisle. On top of his sarcophagus, superbly carved by N.G. von Leiden, a sculptor of the late Middle Ages, is a statue of the emperor accompanied by his emblems. The tomb of Prince Eugene of

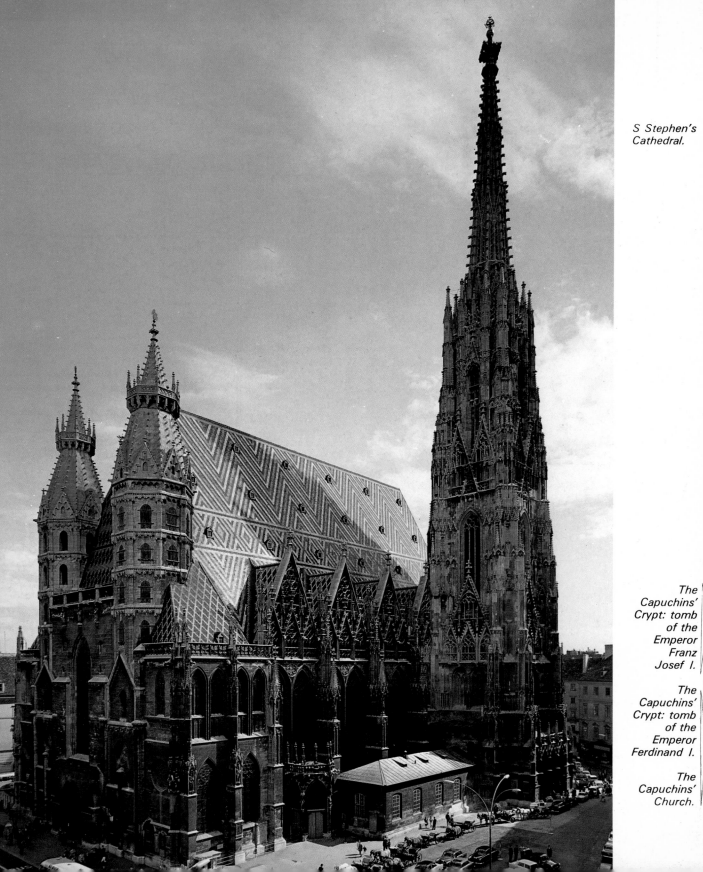

S Stephen's
Cathedral.

The
Capuchins'
Crypt: tomb
of the
Emperor
Franz
Josef I.

The
Capuchins'
Crypt: tomb
of the
Emperor
Ferdinand I.

The
Capuchins'
Church.

Savoy is also interesting. The high altar is particularly remarkable, it is presided over by an image of S Stephen, by Tobias Bock, depicting the stoning of the cathedral's patron saint.

Special mention is also due to the pulpit, constructed in 1510 by Anton Pilgram, who was another of the cathedral's master-builders. Its supporting pillar displays a magnificent self-portrait depicting Pilgram looking through a half-open window. The visitor should also look closely at the figures of four Fathers of the Church that decorate the pulpit. The image of "Our Lady of Domestic Workers" (Dienstboten-madonna), a 16th-century work also by Pilgram, is very beautiful as well.

There is a platform by the side of the "Pummerin" bell — also a distinguishing feature of Vienna — reached by a lift, from which one may enjoy a splendid panorama of the city laid out in all directions, with the foothills of the Alps and beautiful forests on the horizon.

S Stephen's Cathedral was severely damaged during the Soviet Army's offensive launched on the 6th April 1945, which ended in the capture of Vienna on the 13th. Even earlier, however — on the 12th March of the same year — devastating aerial bombardment by United States forces had seriously damaged the Sacristy, on the cathedral's east side. As a result of an intense Soviet attack from the air the houses opposite the main entrance caught fire on the 8th April. When the Soviet army began to enter S Stephen's Square — on the 10th — the retreating German troops shelled the city, opening several holes in the cathedral roof. The fire took hold of the building and extended on the 11th and 12th. The situation was aggravated in consequence of the fact that the Germans had taken Vienna's fire-brigade with them. The fire affected the north tower in particular. The wooden

The interior of S Charles' Church.

"Maria am Gestade"Church.

framework for the bells collapsed into the nave. The whole of the cathedral's interior, including that of one of the Towers of the Pagans, was in flames. The cupola over the choir-stalls and the cathedral's main bell collapsed. On the 13th April the fire's destructive work was accomplished: the greater part of the centre choir's vaulting and that of the lateral choir on the south side had fallen in, while the emperors' oratories and the precious Gothic choir-stalls had been destroyed.

The population of Vienna could only witness in anguish the destruction of the monument that most faithfully symbolised the city's past glories. The Viennese, however, did not resign themselves to merely conserving the image of the cathedral in their memory: they resolved to rebuild it. Otto Stradal wrote: "Thanks to the generosity of Vienna's population and the patient, anonymous labour of architects and stonemasons, the church has been completely restored, assuming once again its original appearance." Only the marvellous stained glass windows have proved impossible to recreate. But the beautiful architectural structure of S Stephen's Cathedral is now re-established.

THE CAPUCHINS' CHURCH AND THE EMPEROR'S TOMB

The Capuchins' Church was endowed by the Empress Anne, the wife of the Emperor Matthias (who died in 1618), but built after her death, from 1622 to 1632; and it was rebuilt in 1936, following the original plans. The building is sober, plain and of little artistic significance, in accordance with the precepts of the Mendicant Orders.

Its importance derives from the Emperor's Tomb, also called the Capuchins' Tomb. This is the Hapsburg family's pantheon, containing 138 metal coffins, in-

"Schottenkirche" Church.

S Peter's Church.

S Rupert's Church.

"Griechenbeisel" restaurant.

cluding those of 12 German or Austrian emperors and 15 empresses. Of the sovereigns after the Emperor Matthias, only two are missing: the Emperor Ferdinand II, under whose mandate the original tomb was constructed — he is buried in Graz — and Karl I, the last Hapsburg emperor, who was laid to rest in Madeira. The sarcophagi are a demonstration of the evolving spirit of the times over three centuries, in close connection with artistic evolution. The range goes from the highest splendour of the period of Maria Theresa, through the restrained style of Josef II, to the renewed monumental grandeur of the second half of the 19th century.

THE CITY

Vienna is in all aspects one of the most interesting cities in Europe. Twenty centuries of distinguished history have gradually formed the old imperial city's spiritual and visual image. Vienna's immense wealth of monuments is accompanied by the charm of a style of life that — without diminishing in the slightest its modern dynamism — conserves a basis of fascinating millenary customs.

In Vienna one may view traces in stone of the Romans' passage, vestiges of Romanesque art, Gothic architecture and baroque mansions, all contributing to the multifarious overall image that characterises the city. This general appearance is also enhanced by the famous woods of Vienna, the fabulous castle and park of Schönbrunn, little vineyards, the roses in the Volksgarten and the unmistakable atmosphere of romantic 19th-century cafés.

The city has an inimitable style of its own, harmoniously combining the spirit of Vienna and its urban appearance: in this style one may perceive the

*The Greeks'
Church.*

The Imperial Palace. (Hofburg).

The "Power of the Sea" fountain. ▷

melodies that Mozart, Liszt, Haydn, Beethoven, Schubert and Brahms composed in Vienna; it is redolent of the golden age of waltzes and operettas written by Lanner, Ziehrer and Strauss. Then, as the pride of Vienna's spirit, there are its many museums, replete with artistic treasures.

S Stephen's is the nerve-centre of the city. The stylised spire of the Gothic cathedral's tower seems to symbolise the spirituality of this metropolis, which was for centuries a bastion of western civilization. S Michael's Square (Michaelerplatz) is not far from S Stephen's, it is reached via the attractive Graben and Kohlmarkt streets. A plaque on the corner of Kohlmarkt street and Michaelerplatz records that, in the middle of the 18th century, a humble garret there

was inhabited by Joseph Haydn: one of the great musical geniuses of Austria, a country that has produced so many exceptional musicians.

Michaelerplatz is one of the most interesting parts of the city. S Michael's Church is located here, it was once the imperial army's sanctuary: a fine 18th-century building retaining a meritorious 14th-century choir.

THE IMPERIAL PALACE

Michaelerplatz is dominated by the majestic façade of the Hofburg, a sumptuous former imperial palace. The forged iron gate in the centre of the façade draws

the visitor's attention; it is flanked by four groups of
sculptures. There is an arched niche in each of the
two wings, with fountains symbolising "the power of
the earth" and "the power of the sea." The centre of
the building is surmounted by a large cupola with, on
the left, the entrance to the celebrated imperial
quarters. These comprise a great audience hall, the
dining-room (where the table is kept exactly as it was
at the time of the Congress of Vienna, when the Czar
Alexander I lived in this part of the palace) and the
rooms of the Emperor Franz Josef and the Empress
Elisabeth. These apartments reflect the atmosphere in
which the imperial couple lived here in their happy
years. The period of misfortune was to come later,
when their son committed suicide and the empress
was assassinated. The rooms' architecture displays
noble proportions, and they are decorated with paintings of considerable value. It seems, nevertheless,
that Franz Josef was a man of simple, conventional
tastes. He lived with the austerity of a soldier and
considered himself the Austro-Hungarian Monarchy's
first civil servant and officer. Visitors are now shown,
as a curiosity, the balcony from which Franz Josef I
used to watch the changing of the guard, hidden
behind the drapes, with his watch in his hand.
After crossing the rotunda of the cupola, one reaches
a courtyard within the palace with, in the centre, the
great monument to the Emperor Franz. The four cor-
ners of the courtyard date from different architectural
periods. The oldest side is the one with the Swiss
Door: painted in remarkable colours, this was built at
the time of the Emperor Ferdinand I, from 1536 to
1552, and is the most important of the few specimens
of the Renaissance in Vienna. The derricks by means
of which the drawbridge was operated, and part of
the old moats, are still conserved. This door leads to
the Swiss Court and the Palace Chapel, which was
built in the middle of the 15th century; only the choir

The Imperial Palace: Swiss Door.

is visible from the outside. On Sundays at 9.30 this is where the famous Child Singers, accompanied by musicians from Vienna Philharmonic Orchestra, perform masterpieces of religious music for mass: this is one of the most beautiful, moving experiences to be had in the city.

A totally exceptional museum has been installed opposite the Hofburg chapel. The sumptuously decorated galleries display a collection of masterpieces of the jeweller's art in gold and silver, of incalculable value, a veritable treasure chamber, dazzling the visitor. This museum — unique the world

The Hofburg: inner courtyard with the statue to the Emperor Franz I.

The Child Singers of Vienna.

over — is divided into a gallery for liturgical treasure and another for secular works. Special attention should be paid to the coronation insignia of the Holy Roman-Germanic emperors, those which made up Maximilian I's Burgundian treasure, the jewels that belonged to the Empress Maria Theresa, the magnificent outfit adorned with precious stones in which the Emperor Franz Josef I was baptised, superb tunics of the Order of the Golden Fleece and the crown — studded with precious stones — used by the emperors of Austria from Redbeard's reign to that of Franz I. Furthermore: coronation robes, Maria Theresa's golden rose, the nail from Christ's cross — brought to Vienna at the time of the Crusades — and a vast array of fabrics encrusted with pearls, and suits

embroidered in gold. In this museum the visitor may also admire the priceless reliquaries and other articles comprising the ecclesiastical treasure, and the king of Rome's cradle.

Returning to the palace's marvellous interior courtyard, the visitor can view the three other sides. The Amalia Palace (Amalienburg), standing opposite the Swiss Door, is in the early baroque style: it was begun under the Emperor Maximilian in 1575 and completed by the Emperor Rudolf II in 1611. Leopold I's wing is on the west side of the courtyard, he built it from 1660 to 1666; after a fire it was restored by Ludwig Burnacini from 1668 to 1670. The court's principal side, in the late baroque style, is a wing accommodating the Royal Chancellory, built from 1723 to 1730 — in the

Treasure Museum: crown of the Holy Roman-Germanic Empire.

reign of Karl VI — by Johann Lukas von Hildebrandt and Josef Emanuel Fischer von Erlach.

A passageway in the Leopold Wing leads to the Square of Heroes (Heldenplatz), where there are two equestrian statues. One depicts the Prince of Savoy, who was in command of the Austrian troops that defended Vienna from the Turks' attacks; the other statue is of the Archduke Karl, who led the resistance against Napoleon's invasion. The area known as the New Hofburg forms a broad semicircle giving onto the Heldenplatz and the attractive groves of the Volksgarten. This is one of the most beautiful parks in Vienna. History mingles with art here, making it possible for one's imagination to conjure up the imperial city's splendid past.

The official residence of the president of the Austrian Republic is now in the Leopold Wing, where the Empress Maria Theresa formerly had her private rooms. All her prime ministers lived in the white baroque building opposite, which is now the seat of the Federal Chancellory.

THE RIDING SCHOOL

Continuing from Michaelerplatz towards the Opera House, the visitor can reach the Court Riding School (Reitschule), where the Hapsburgs' famous stables with Lipizzaners from the Spanish court's Riding School (Picadero) are to be found.

The construction of the Reitschule began in 1728,

Treasure Museum: the Hapsburgs' crown.

following plans drawn up by Fischer von Erlach; it was concluded by his son in 1735. The building was used as a winter riding school. There is a gallery supported by sixteen Corinthian columns. The Spanish Riding School is the only one in the world where classical horsemanship is practised; it was founded by Karl VI. The Spanish horse — a combination of Hispanic and Arab blood — was introduced into Austria in 1580, when the first specimens arrived at Lipizza, now part of Yugoslavia. The movements of the ''emperor's white horses'' — as they are still known — are a very attractive sight. The exhibition of classical horsemanship by the white stud horses and their trainers constitutes a colourful cameo of old, imperial Vienna. The white chargers — with gold threads gleaming in their manes — are ridden by horsemen who still wear the characteristic imperial costume: red dress coats with golden adornments and white cuffs (or brown coats with black silk cuffs), white leather trousers, tall shining boots of patent-leather, two-cornered hats with golden cockades, and Spanish daggers. Lit by the gallery's chandeliers, the horses and riders commence the exhibition, which is based on elegant prances, extraordinarily fine skipping movements (which at times recall the tapping heels of a good Spanish dancer) and pretended rearings-up…. At a certain moment the splendid white horses begin to dance with inimitable elegance, while an orchestra plays minuet, polka or slow waltz music.

The dining-room inside the Imperial Palace.

Josef II Square (Josefsplatz), with an equestrian statue of the emperor, is near the Riding School. The square is surrounded by several fine buildings in the baroque style, in particular the National Library — with extraordinarily valuable collections— which was built by Fischer von Erlach the Younger in 1723, following plans drawn up by his father; and the Albertina, an important museum conserving some 30,000 drawings and 50,000 engravings by great universal masters of painting, especially Dürer, Rembrandt and Rubens.

By proceeding from Josefsplatz towards the Opera House the visitor will reach the Ring, the famous boulevard — flanked by magnificent parks and lavish buildings — that came into being in the middle of the 19th century when Vienna's ramparts were demolished so as to allow the city to expand.

THE RING

This attractive boulevard encircles the centre of Vienna, running through part of the old city, criss-

crossed by winding streets full of history. The Ring encloses what was the heart of Vienna in the second half of the 19th century. Today it is a sumptuous street symbolising imperial Austria in its historic grandeur, when Vienna was, like Paris, the Europeans' city of dreams.

The Opera House is in the Ring, which is the same as saying the musical centre of the world; for Austria is the home of music and Vienna was — is — the capital city of Europe as regards music. The Austrian nation has always been so closely associated with music that — apart from the innumerable musicians of genius born in Austria, many of them in Vienna itself — there were even three emperors who were also composers: Ferdinand III, Leopold I and Josef I. The first-mentioned of these was the author of *Drama Musicum,* a fragment of which Athanasius Kircher — the Jesuit to whom the opera is dedicated — included

Inside the Imperial Palace: a room for conversation.

Imperial Palace: the IAEA meeting-room.

in his composition *Musurgia Universalis.* Ferdinand III composed a madrigal, a mass and ten hymns, among other musical works. Another composer/emperor was Leopold I, the more outstanding of his compositions are the operettas *Die vermeinte Bruder und Schwesterliebe, Der törichte Schäfer* and *Die Sklavinnen von Samia.* He further composed 79 religious works, 155 songs for one or several voices, 17 suites for ballet and 9 operas: Leopold I was, without a doubt, the most prolific of the Austrian emperors who dedicated themselves to music. Josef I, however, is considered to have been the emperor of the greatest musical talent. His works include seven religious and lay compositions for singing and a piece for the lute. Karl VI was also a composer. The Empress Maria Theresa performed as a singer in Court

perfomances. Her son Josef II was a pupil of Florian Leopold Gassmann — the Court Orchestra's conductor — and played the piano and the cello, sometimes singing. Franz I organized concerts in Laxenburg castle. The Archduke Rudolf von Hapsburg wrote some compositions and was Beethoven's pupil and friend; and even the Emperor Franz Josef I had lessons in music and acting. Vienna was for a considerable period the world's musical capital, and the Opera House, a kind of sanctuary for the most important musical events.

One of the most dynamic shopping-centres in Vienna is located in the Opernpassage. Pedestrians can cross under the intersection of the Ring and Kärntnerstrasse — always very busy with dense traffic — by means of escalators. There is a real underground

Van Gogh: The Antwerp Plain *(Neue Galerie in der Stallburg).*

Van Gogh: Self-portrait *(Neue Galerie in der Stallburg).*

city here, with department stores, luxurious shops, information offices, cafeterias, bookshops, pastry-shops, and many other establishments which are open both in the daytime and at night. The most important hotels in Vienna are not far from the Opera House, among them the Sacher — famous for its cake — and the Imperial. The former was the preferred haunt of the aristocracy of the Austro-Hungarian Empire before the first World War and the stylish setting of its salons was often used as the background for well-known period films. The Imperial Hotel stands on the Ring Avenue, by Schwarzenberg square: the most prominent politicians of central Europe have stayed in its rooms. These famous ''princes' lodgings'' were occupied by heads of government at the time of the monarchy; today they are generally frequented by famous artists, oil magnates, powerful financiers and other distinguished personages.

Renoir: The Blonde Bather *(Neue Galerie in der Stallburg).*

The Fine Arts
Museum and statue of
Maria Theresa.

*Imperial Palace
(Hofburg).*

*The Natural History
Museum and statue of
the Archduke Karl.*

Imperial Palace: stairway, music room and armour room.

The National Library. ▷

The House of Parliament is another important building situated on the Ring, it was built by the Danish architect Theophil von Hansen, in the Greek Revival style, in 1883.

The neo-Gothic City Hall is nearby; its tower, some 100 metres in height, is surmounted by a copper statue 3.49 m high, weighing 3.6 tonnes, which depicts a Viennese soldier, armed and bearing the flag. The inhabitants of Vienna jokingly call this figure "the man from the City Hall." The Reception Hall and the Municipal Library are worth visiting. Vienna's City Hall building is the majestic setting for the opening and closure ceremonies of the city's Festival Weeks, which are held in June and constitute the most impressive cultural event of the year.

FINE ARTS MUSEUM

One of the greatest attractions of Vienna is constituted by its numerous important museums, amongst which the Fine Arts Museum (Kunsthistorisches Museum) — also located on the Ring — is outstanding. Its exhibits, on show in the main building, comprise splendid art collections: particularly remarkable are the section of paintings (on the Ist floor), that of plastic arts, and craft work (on the left of the mezzanine), the carved stones (right mezzanine) and the collection of coins (2nd floor), considered to be one of the most important in the world. There are a total of 91 rooms, of all sizes, in the building: a complete visit means walking more than four kilometres. The collections come from the art treasures of the principalities of Vienna, Graz, Brussels, Prague and Innsbruck.

The Hapsburg dynasty's treasure can be traced back to the late 13th century; it formed the basis of the Emperor Ferdinand I's important collection. Ferdinand bequeathed this to his sons the Emperor Max-

Fine Arts Museum: the Decorative Arts Room.

Fine Arts Museum: the Emperor Josef I and the Amazons' sarcophagus; and a gallery of the Natural History Museum.

imilian II, Duke Ferdinand of Tyrol and the Archduke Karl of Steiermark. The Emperor Rudolf II combined the Emperor Ferdinand of Tyrol's collection with his own, which he transferred from Prague to Vienna. Before that, however — in 1667 — the Gallery of the Archduke Leopold Wilhelm, a städtholder of the Netherlands, had enriched the emperor's art treasure; and in 1765, under Maria Theresa, the Graz treasure was incorporated into that at Vienna. The collections were brought together in the present-day building in 1889. The museum's stocks grew by means of pur-

chases, donations and excavations, until it comprised 480,000 pieces; with the result that part of the collection had to be stored elsewhere.

The most valuable collection, by virtue of its unity, is probably that of paintings by Pieter Bruegel, the Dutch painter: the Kunsthistorisches Museum possesses the largest number of his canvases in any one place. Other outstanding works include those by Anton van Dyck — his *Samson and Delilah* is a large canvas, with baroque influences — and Titian, *Diana and Calixtus;* Albrecht Dürer — *Adoration of the Holy*

Fine Arts Museum: Egyptian art.

Fine Arts Museum: The Virgin Mary and Child.

Trinity; Velázquez — *Portrait of the Infanta Margarita Teresa in a blue dress;* and Rubens — *Portrait of Hélène Fourment, Lamentation for the Dead Christ* and, above all, *The Fur Coat,* a canvas of regular size painted in 1638, depicting a nude woman, her body shining with pearly tones, covering her back and abdomen with a fur coat. This is a daringly sensual work and reveals the expressive genius of this famous German artist of the Flemish school. The gallery also has masterpieces by Raphael, Rembrandt, van Eyck, Lukas Cranach and many other great masters.

The other nine sections of the Fine Arts Museum are equally interesting: the collections of Oriental and Egyptian art; antiques; plastic arts and craft work; medals, coins and monetary units; musical instruments; weapons; and the museum of Austrian culture.

It is a feast both for the eyes and for the spirit to visit the Fine Arts Museum in Vienna. The ensemble of works that may be admired in the different galleries — their installation is nothing short of model — is extremely impressive. The paintings and other pieces collected together here give an idea of the important rôle the capital of Vienna played in Europe's cultural life. It has been stated, not unjustly, that in relation to its geographical extension Austria possesses more masterpieces, both in painting and in sculpture, than any other country in the world, with the exception of the Vatican. The tour of the Museum's galleries not only stimulates the visitor's sensibility but also allows

Fine Arts Museum: interior.

Pieter
Bruegel:
Wedding
Banquet
(Fine Arts
Museum).

Anton van
Dyck:
Samson and
Delilah (Fine
Arts
Museum).

Fine Arts Museum: The Tower of Babel *by Pieter Bruegel;* Diana and Calixtus *by Titian;* Portrait of the Infanta Margarita Teresa at the age of eight *by Velázquez; and* Adoration of the Holy Trinity *by Albrecht Dürer.*

Rubens: The Fur Coat *(Fine Arts Museum).*

one's imagination to fly and relive the past by means of the magic of these works of art; the ensemble reveals the exceptional spirit of a country with extraordinary conditions for the cultivation of artistic creation in all its facets and nuances, and also demonstrates that the Austrian people are inclined to conserve and protect all these art treasures. Nobody can deny Vienna the title of the capital of music, but at the same time it is one of the cities where painting is considered as the expression of cultural advances.

ALBERTINA MUSEUM

Vienna is a paradise for museum-goers. As well as the Fine Arts Museum already mentioned, and the magnificent collections in the Belvedere, there are many other museums in Austria's capital city: for example, the Ethnological Museum, the Hackney-Carriages Museum, the Funeral Museum, the Natural History Museum, the Museum of Viticulture; and those devoted to Beethoven, Haydn, Mozart, Schubert and Albert Stifter. The city also caters, however, for the devotee of small museums. These include the Historical Museum of the City of Vienna located in Karlsplatz, the Museum of Applied Arts with its remarkable clocks, carpets and antique porcelain, the Circus Museum, the Fashion Museum, the Museum of Typical Viennese Sweets in an old bakery in Langegasse, and the collection that may be visited in the charming Geymüller palace in Pötzleinsdorf....
The Albertina Museum is, however, one of the most

Rubens' Lamentation for the Dead Christ *and Raphael's* The Virgin Mary with S John and the Child Jesus *(Fine Arts Museum).*

important. The building, raised as the Silva-Taroucca Palace in 1781, was enlarged from 1801 to 1804 — and part of the neighbouring Augustinian monastery was incorporated — following plans by Luis de Montoyer, for the Archduke Karl, who defeated Napoleon I in the Battle of Aspern and was the Archduke Albert's father. In 1822 Josef Kornhäusl adapted the interior to the classical style.

The building's present appearance is a result of rebuilding work after 1945, when the great outside stairway was added. Since 1795, this palace — then the residence of the Archduchess Maria Cristina and her husband, the Archduke Albert of Saxony-Teschen — has housed the world-famous collection of drawings and graphic prints that they acquired.

Prince Eugene of Savoy's collection constitutes a fundamental part of the museum. The Albertina's collection of graphic art — with 40,000 drawings and more than 1,000,000 plates, engravings, etchings and lithographs — is the largest and most important in the world; and is constantly being expanded. It includes works from all countries and schools. Special mention should be made — among the German schools of the 16th century — of the drawings by Albrecht Dürer, Hans Holbein, Jörg Breu, Lukas Cranach, Peter Altdorfer and many others. The Dutch school is also represented — by Pieter Bruegel, Lukas von Falkenborch and Anton van Dyck — as are the great Italian masters: Raphael, Veronese, Guardi and Canaletto. Since the space required makes it impossible to present all these works simultaneously, a different part of the museum's collection is exhibited each year.

The Albertina Museum.

MONUMENTS IN VIENNA

Austria's capital city is extraordinarily rich in monuments. There are not only buildings famous for their historical significance — such as S Stephen's Cathedral, the Imperial Palace (Hofburg), the City Hall, the Belvedere or Schönbrunn — but also numerous statues in honour of different personages, scattered over the whole city.

Among the most popular statues in Vienna, that of Marshal Radetzky, in the Ringstrasse, is outstanding; this officer was a famous military leader in imperial Austria, and Johann Strauss the Elder dedicated the lively piece known as the Radetzky March to him. Other important sights are the bust of Wolfgang Amadeus Mozart, the celebrated composer, located in the Hofburg gardens; the ''An der Wein'' theatre's portico, adorned by a depiction in stone of Emmanuel Schikaneder, author of the libretto of *The Magic Flute;* and there is a monument to Johann Strauss the Younger in the City Park. The Column of the Plague, also dedicated to the Holy Trinity, stands in Graben: It was built between 1682 and 1693, in the time of the Emperor Leopold I; the emperor thus fulfilled the promise he had made when the plague ravaged the city in 1679. The monument to Liebenberg — opposite the University — was raised to commemorate the heroic rôle played by the students during the Turkish attack in 1683; Liebenberg, the mayor of Vienna who led the students, died during the struggle. The Hoher Markt is the oldest square in Vienna, its site was occupied of old by the Roman forum: the monument known as the Wedding Column was built there, in honour of the Virgin Mary's wedding, by J.E. Fischer von Erlach from 1729 to 1732. Then there are the monumental "Danube" fountain, depicting this and other principal rivers of Austria, next to the old Augustinians' Bastion behind the Opera House; the monument to the Archduke Albert — commemorating the Austrian victory at Custozza — opposite the Albertina Museum; the monumental fountain depicting Pallas Athene, by C. Kundmann, opposite the Parliament; the monuments to Schiller and Goethe.... The relation of interesting monuments existent in Vienna, erected in honour of illustrious personages or to commemorate glorious historical events, could be continued indefinitely. It would be no exaggeration to say that, really, the whole of Vienna is a monument.

Over and above the palaces and statues already mentioned, the capital of Austria offers the visitor who contemplates its streets and squares the charming architecture of its churches: for example, S Charles' is a masterpiece of the baroque style, built by Fischer von Erlach from 1716 to 1737. The columns outside the church depict the life of S Charles Borromeo; valuable paintings by Ricci and by Daniel Gran are kept inside. Also the 14th-century Gothic church of Maria am Gestade; and the Votive Church (Votivkirche), built on the initiative of the Archduke Maximilian — later to become the unfortunate emperor of Mexico — which is a reminder of the unsuccessful attempt to assassinate the Emperor Franz Josef I in 1853, for it was built (according to a design by Heinrich von Ferst) on the very site of the attack. This is considered to be the most important neo-Gothic building in Vienna. The exterior walls are built of limestone and contain 78 paintings on glass, by Geyerling, decorating the windows. The illumination of the church at night highlights the subtle elements of its structure, based on the canons of the French Gothic style of the 13th-14th centuries. The flying buttress by the choir is particularly effective.

S Rupert's is the oldest church in the city: it was founded in the 8th century and has been restored several times, but conserves Romanesque and Gothic

The Albertina Museum.

"Fiaker" or coaches.

Three views of the "Fiaker".

elements in its architecture. There is also a magnificent painting, by Michael Rotmeier, on the high altar. "Am Hof" church is Gothic in style, dating from the late 14th and early 15th centuries, and was rebuilt first after a fire in 1607-10 and again in 1662, when Carlo Antonio Carlone designed the fine baroque façade.

The cloister of the Monastery of the Holy Cross is another remarkable sight. The monastery was built from 1659 to 1676 and transformed throughout the 18th century.

There are a number of other buildings in Vienna's built-up area that are especially interesting for their architectural design, or historical value, or because they are typical of Viennese charm. Mention should be made here of the popular "Greek Tavern" (Griechenbeisel), one of the oldest, most fascinating Greek restaurants in the Fleischmarkt; of the many Viennese cafés, symbols of a splendid, romantic period, the era of the popular master of the waltz, Strauss; and of numerous houses in the baroque style, as also the charming taverns in the Grinzing area.

Loos House merits mention as well: in Michaelerplatz, its architect was Adolf Loos, one of the pioneers of Austrian Modernism.

The University is another oustanding sight, the present-day building was built by Ferstel from 1874 to 1883. Vienna University — *Alma Mater Rudolfina* — was founded by Rudolf IV in the mid-14th century. There is a small square opposite the building conserving remains of the old ramparts, where the Turks concentrated their attacks in 1683. The Prince of Ligne, Friedrich von Gentz and Beethoven all lived here in the period between the Congress of Vienna and the 1848 revolution; and the popular "House of the three maidens" (Dreimäderlhaus) is here too. The City Hall Square (Rathausplatz) is another obligatory tourist sight, Vienna's City Hall building — mentioned earlier — stands here: its style is neo-Gothic, with some Renaissance features, and it was built from 1872 to 1883, following plans by the architect Friedrich Schmidt. Popular concerts are held in its colonnaded courtyard in summer.

Detail of the City Hall.

City Hall: the Council Room.

The City Hall.

The National Theatre.

THE BURGTHEATER

Of the numerous theatres in Vienna, we should highlight — as well as the State Opera and the Burgtheater — the theatre of the People's Opera in Währingerstrasse, the Academy Theatre in Lisztstrasse, the "Theater an der Wein" in Linke Wienzeile, the Chamber Theatre in Rotenturmstrasse, the "Theater an der Josefstadt" in Josefstädterstrasse, the People's Theatre in Neustiftgasse, the Small Theatre of the Concert Palace in Lothringerstrasse, the English Theatre of Vienna in Josefgasse, the Raimund Theatre in Wallgasse, the Chamber Opera House of Vienna in Fleischmarkt and the Small Comedy in the Archduke Karl's Palace, situated in Annagasse. In addition to these State and private theatres, there are also a good number of smaller theatres, such as "The Actors," the "Courage Theatre," or the "Tribune" or "Studio" Theatre in Naschmarkt.

The National Theatre (Burgtheater, popularly shortened to "the Burg") is one of the oldest, most traditional stages in the world, and the most celebrated theatre of the German-speaking countries. As early as 1741 it was installed, with Maria Theresa's permission, in Michaelerplatz, in a former ballroom of the emperor's residence; in 1888 it was transferred to the present building, which is by G. Semper and K. Hasenauer. With directors as famous as Josef Schreyvogel and Heinrich Laube, the Burgtheater soon attained its position as the preponderant stage of the German language. Tribute is paid to the famous poets associated with this building, and to outstanding personages of the world of the theatre, by statues placed in the different façades of the theatre. The building was destroyed in a fire in 1945 and entirely rebuilt from 1951 to 1955.

*The main
staircase of
the National
Theatre.*

The State Opera House: façade and views of the interior.

The Great Ball at the Opera House.

THE STATE OPERA HOUSE

The State Opera — previously the Court Opera and to this day one of the foremost opera houses in the world — was built from 1861 to 1869. The plans were by August von Siccardsburg — as architect of the whole — and Eduard van der Nüll — who designed the interior — in conformance with the historical style of the Florentine/French Early Renaissance. The building was inaugurated in 1869 with Mozart's opera *Don Giovanni*. The two architects were so heavily criticised that they were unable to attend the première. Van der Nüll committed suicide and, two months later, Siccardsburg had a heart attack. Neither the populace nor the Court liked the building's style: this, in conjunction with the burlesque verses that the Viennese dedicated to Siccardsburg's and Van der Nüll's bad taste, may have been the cause of their tragic deaths.

The Opera House was hit by bombs on the 12th March, 1945, and caught fire: only the balcony, foyer, main stairway and a tea-room survived. It was rebuilt from 1948 to 1955, following plans — very similar to the original design — drawn up by Erich Bolternstern, Otto Possinger and Zeno Kossak, architects. In 1955 the Opera House on the Ring reopened its doors with a performance of Beethoven's *Fidelio*, conducted by Karl Böhm. The great artistic achievements of the opera in Vienna are based on a permanent company, which includes many world-renowned stars, and above all on the high musical standard of the Opera House orchestra, strengthened by members of the Vienna Philharmonic Orchestra. Great musicians have been conductors here: Gustav Mahler, Richard Strauss, Franz Schalk, Clemens Krauss, Herbert von

The Parliament building, with the monument to Pallas Athene.

Karajan and Karl Böhm have given the State Opera the artistic stimulus that corresponds to its class. The Opera House has a capacity for 2,209 spectators, with an area of 9,000 sq.m. The orchestra pit accommodates 110 musicians. The building has two halls for ballet rehearsals, three for the performers' company, a stage for rehearsals, ten rooms for rehearsing solos, an organ room and another where fifty microphones can be connected for radio broadcasts. There are also nine relays for televison. The Opera House consumes an amount of electricity equivalent to the requirements of a city of 30,000 inhabitants.

PARLIAMENT

The Parliament building was constructed in the Greek Revival style from 1874 to 1883, following plans drawn up by Theophil von Hansen. The centre of the pediment depicts the Emperor Franz Josef's granting of the Constitution. There are several statues on a ramp, depicting Greek and Roman sages; and also four horse-breakers at its end, sculptured in bronze by Lax. The Fountain Monument depicting the Greek goddess Pallas Athene, raised by Kundmann in 1902, stands opposite the Parliament.

FRIENDS OF MUSIC SOCIETY

The Musikverein, founded by a group of music-lovers in 1812, above all organizes concerts and musical evenings. From 1867 to 1869 the Society commissioned Theophil von Hansen to build new premises for its Music School and for the promotion of musical arts. The Conservatory is one of the oldest institutions where music is taught. The organization has very important archives conserving valuable editions of musical works and original manuscripts by great composers. The collection of musical instruments from different periods is also of great interest. The main room, the famous "Golden Salon," is reached by crossing the lavish stair-well. With its dimensions of 51.2 metres long, 18.9 m wide and 17.6 m high, this concert hall is considered to have the best acoustic conditions of any in the world; it seats 2,000 people.

Concert Hall (Musikverein).

Kärntnerstrasse.

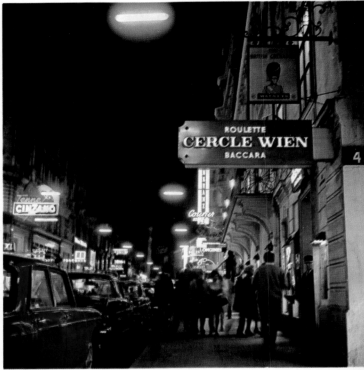

Kärntnerstrasse.

The "Moulin Rouge."

Mariahilferstrasse.

The Ring. The Imperial Hotel.

Shop-windows.

VIENNA'S FASCINATING SHOPS

It is a real pleasure to go shopping in Vienna. Kärntnerstrasse, Graben and Kohlmarkt (an exclusively pedestrian zone), situated in the city centre, constitute a constant temptation for the visitor. The most elegant shops in the city, with their dazzling window-displays, are located here. In the old part of Vienna there are also many boutiques, fascinating galleries and small bazaars dotting the charming little streets, where it is difficult to resist the temptation to buy. Devotees of antiques will be captivated by the Second-Hand Market and also by the "Dorotheum" — a former State pawnshop — where important auctions of objets d'art and diverse antiques are held.

The products of Vienna's craftsmen are very attractive: a demonstration of the traditional good taste of the city's artisans. Among the particularly enticing objects we would mention Vienna's Augarten porcelain, hand-made dolls, artistic ceramic pieces, wrought iron objects, enamels, leather articles and jewellery.

Fashion in Vienna enjoys a long-standing, well earned reputation: the city's haute couture produces singularly elegant clothes. There is also an accredited Fashion School, accommodated in Hetzendorf Palace.

"Viennese style" furniture is also highly appreciated; today it is produced in designs faithful to the original models.

PARKS OF VIENNA

Vienna is a city that has succeeded, in spite of its expansion, in conserving extensive areas of parks and gardens: around 1,700 hectares of green spaces within the city limits. There are numerous excellent parks scattered all over the city. Not far from the Hofburg, in the Burggarten, stands the monument to Wolfgang Amadeus Mozart, one of the greatest musical geniuses born in Austria. Another monument surrounded by Vienna's green gardens — the Stadtpark — is the one raised in honour of Johann Strauss, who was born in Vienna in 1825 and, in the triumphant course of his lifetime, composed 496 major works including such outstanding operettas as *Die Fledermaus* ("The Bat"), *Der Zigeunerbaron* ("The Gypsy Baron"), and waltzes as famous as *The Blue Danube.* The Strauss monument was built by

The University and the statue of Liebenberg.

The monument dedicated to Mozart.

Johann Strauss.

The large City Park.

Volksgarten.

Edmund Hellmer; the popular Viennese musican is shown surrounded by beautiful Danubian undines.

In the Floridsdorf quarter, on the other side of the Danube, there are garden cafés with large, verdant parks.

In 1964, on the occasion of the International Gardening Exhibition organized in Vienna, the Danube Tower (Donauturm) was constructed: it is 252 m high. The Donauturm is situated in a recreational park between the Danube and the Old Danube. There is a revolving café on its terrace, from which one may enjoy a splendid, vast panorama over Vienna: on a clear day it is even possible to descry the Hungarian border. As well as the elegant Belvedere and Schönbrunn gardens, special mention is due to those of the Prater (formerly a hunting reserve for the exclusive use of the imperial family and the nobility, opened by the Emperor Josef II in 1766): one of the most beautiful parks in Vienna, with extensive meadowlands and abundant woods. It is also equipped with super-modern sporting installations — such as the famous stadium, racecourses and several swimming-pools — and includes the Nature Park, formed by Gänsehäufel island, and the Danube Park, a densely frequented watering place where all kinds of water sports are practised.

Beyond the Prater fun fair and the woodland of the Danube Park stretch the marvellous wooded areas that surround Vienna on the west side: this green zone is named Wienerwald and links Vienna with the north-east foothills of the Alps.

GRABEN

Graben is — with Kohlmarkt and Kärntnerstrasse — one of the most distinguished streets in Vienna. Its name is derived from the trenches (in German,

Graben, with the Column of the Plague.

Festigungsgraben) existent there from Roman times until the middle of the 12th century, which marked the western boundary of the city. The trenches were filled in, and houses built on the site, when Leopold VI the Glorious extended the city in 1225. Graben was a bustling market street: a food market used to be held there and, from 1702 onwards, this was supplemented by the ''Glückshäfen'' — stalls for games of chance — and shops selling gold and silver plate. In the reign of Maria Theresa this became the centre of big-city life: not only the elegant place to stroll in Vienna, but also the meeting-place of the famous Graben courtesans, members of Vienna's underworld.

This part of the city is dominated by the Column of the Plague, dedicated to the Holy Trinity, erected on Leopold I's orders by way of thanksgiving for the end of the devastating plague of 1679. The artists involved in creating the monument included Burnacini and Rauchmiller; the basic conception of the column is due to Johann Bernhard Fischer von Erlach, who intervened in 1687, after the work had been begun, and sculptured the bas-relief. In 1804 Johann Martin Fischer designed the fountains on either side of the Column of the Plague: S Joseph's fountain depicts the saint bending over towards one of the children who hold the family tree; while S Leopold's fountain features a figure of the Babenbergs' patron saint, Leopold III. On the corner of Graben and Kärntnerstrasse the visitor will see a niche with a log called ''the Iron Staff,'' perforated by hundreds of nails. This is said to be the master-work of a certain locksmith, achieved with the help of the devil. After the craftsman perished, the victim of his pact, all the skilled locksmiths and blacksmiths who passed by were obliged to hammer a nail into the log and say a prayer for the wretch.

Hoher Markt.

*A singular clock
(Ankeruhr).*

The secondhand market.

Various views of the secondhand market. ▷

VIENNESE FOLKLORE

Vienna, a city with an illustrious history, has succeeded in conserving its traditional human characteristics in spite of the passage of time and the changes brought by progress. The people of Vienna maintain to this day the age-old custom of frequenting the *Heurigen,* picturesque taverns on the outskirts of the city, where the delicious wine of Austria is drunk, the cultivation of which was introduced into the country by the Romans. Typical restaurants abound in the old quarters. The "Griechenbeisel" is one of the most famous, situated in an area where many shopkeepers of Greek origin have opened establishments, nowadays very popular with artists. The Secondhand Market, in Naschmarkt, is a picturesque sight. The colourful market is teeming and animated every Saturday. An infinite variety of objects is sold at its open-air stalls: from a rickety chair to paintings, engravings, lamps, the most diverse furniture and even real antiques. Another picturesque detail of street life in Vienna is the "marroni stalls," where tasty roast chestnuts are sold in autumn and winter.

The Clocks Museum.

The 20th Century Museum.

CLOCKS MUSEUM, MUSEUM OF THE 20TH CENTURY, ARMY MUSEUM AND TECHNICAL MUSEUM

Vienna is a city with a wealth of important museums. Apart from the artistic treasures kept in the former Imperial Palace, the Fine Arts Museum, the Albertina, in the Austrian Baroque Museum — in the Lower Belvedere — or in the Austrian Gallery of the 19th and 20th Centuries — in the Upper Belvedere — we should also mention the undoubtable interest of other museums. The Clocks Museum of the City of Vienna is at no. 2 Schulhof, and has more than 3,000 pieces; the most outstanding is a magnificent collection of Viennese clocks of all ages. The 20th Century Museum, in the Schweizergarten, has a valuable stock of works of the present century. The Army Museum's galleries illustrate for the visitor all Austria's military history, with different uniforms used in centuries past and a varied collection of arms. The Technical Museum conserves diverse pieces, in particular industrial exhibits.

S CHARLES' CHURCH

The church dedicated to S Charles Borromeo is one of the most handsome baroque churches in Vienna. In 1713, when the city was scourged by the plague for the seventh time, the Emperor Karl VI vowed he would raise a church in honour of the Saint of the Plague. After the rapid extinction of the epidemic, Johann Bernhard Fischer von Erlach commenced work on building S Charles' Church in 1716; it was not completed — by his son Joseph Emanuel — until 1737.

The church displays a cupola of solid design (72 metres) and is — with the sole exception of S Stephen's — the most significant in Vienna. The façade facing the city centre is presided over by two colossal Doric columns, 47 m high, both surmounted

The Army Museum.

by lanterns, that stand in front on either side. These are copies of the columns that Trajan and Marcus Aurelius ordered built in Rome. The socles feature bas-reliefs depicting the life, miracles and death of S Charles. We should also make particular reference to the retable by Daniel Gran, showing Christ informing the Roman centurion that his slave was cured; and to the frescoes in the cupola, by Johann Michael Rottmeyer.

BELVEDERE PALACE

Belvedere Palace was the Prince of Savoy's summer residence. When his mother, Olimpia Mancini, had to flee to Brussels, Eugene — who had been born in Paris — was entrusted to the care of his grandmother, the Princess of Carignan. The prince wanted to dedicate himself to a military career, but Louis XIV was determined that he should pursue the ecclesiastical vocation. This induced Eugene of Savoy to offer his services to the Emperor Leopold I in 1683. Under Charles of Lorraine's command, the prince fought the Turkish troops in the siege of Vienna. He later participated in various campaigns and was seriously wounded in the capture of Belgrade. After being promoted to the rank of marshal, in 1697 he

The Army Museum.

Technical Museum.

was named commander-in-chief of the imperial army which was then engaged in combat with the Turks. He obtained numerous victories and became an extremely well-loved personage among the people of Vienna. His popularity finally made Eugene of Savoy nothing less than a symbol of Austrian resistance to the Turkish incursions. In 1697 he was relieved of the command of the imperial troops, but a demonstration by the people of Vienna obliged the emperor to restore him to this position. His prestige spread all over Europe. After he was named supreme commander of the imperial armies in 1706, Peter the Great offered him the throne of Poland; Eugene of Savoy, however, declined the honour. We owe to this prince the construction of the palaces of Belvedere and Him-

melpfortgasse; and he was the patron of the German philosopher Gottfried Wilhelm Leibnitz and also of Jean-Jacques Rousseau, the celebrated French author of *The Social Contract.*

Belvedere Palace was also the residence of the Archduke Franz Ferdinand, the eldest son of the Archduke Karl Ludwig, the Emperor Franz Josef I's brother. When the Archduke Rudolf, crown prince of the Austro-Hungarian empire, died in Mayerling in 1889 and the Archduke Karl Ludwig also died, in 1896, Franz Ferdinand — being the Emperor Franz Josef's nearest relation — became his heir. After marrying countess Sofia Chotek, who was not received at the Court, Franz Ferdinand renounced his right to the succession. His relationship with the emperor cooled,

Technical Museum.

Belvedere Palace: interior.

Belvedere Palace: façade.

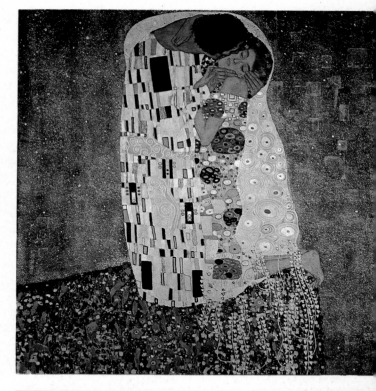

Gustav Klimt: The Lovers.

Belvedere Palace: the marble Gala Hall.

although he did not cease to participate in affairs of State. The archduke was a fervent centralist and, as such, a sworn enemy of the planned Great Serbia. The assassination of the Archduke Franz Ferdinand and his wife in Sarajevo, on the 28th June 1914, unleashed the outbreak of the first World War.

Belvedere Palace is considered to be one of the masterpieces of secular architecture in the baroque style. The famous palace comprises two fine buildings separated by a splendid garden which is, in turn, adorned with artistic statues, elegant fountains and many-coloured flower-beds. A broad, beautiful panorama of Vienna may be enjoyed from the Belvedere, with a splendid vista of the heights of Wienerwald outlined on the horizon.

The building known as the Lower Belvedere, where the Austrian Baroque Museum is now installed, was Prince Eugene of Savoy's real residence. When the Upper Belvedere — now housing the Austrian Gallery of the 19th and 20th Centuries — was built, it was a lavish pavilion where the dazzling festivities of the empire's golden age were held.

Once the visitor has passed through the wrought iron gate, he enters the first garden, with a monumental fountain; while the façade on the opposite side gives onto the park. The land surrounding Belvedere Palace is lovingly cared for and constitutes one of the most stylish gardens in Europe. In 1760 Bellotto painted a famous canvas of the magnificent landscape visible from the Upper Belvedere.

There are several sumptuously decorated salons inside the Upper Belvedere; the most outstanding is the Gala Hall where representatives of Austria, the United States, the Soviet Union, Great Britain and France signed — on the 15th May 1955 — the treaty which put an end to ten years of occupation and restored to the Austrians the independence they had lost when Nazi Germany annexed the historic country's territory in 1938.

Schönbrunn Palace: the Gloriette.

SCHÖNBRUNN

This is one of the most characteristic monuments in Vienna. Around 300 years ago, the area that is now the park of Schönbrunn Palace was occupied by dense woods sheltering abundant species of game. Before that, Katter Mill was here, it is mentioned in documents as early as 1311; a small castle named Katter was built by its side in 1471. Maximilian II acquired the property in 1568, had the buildings converted into a hunting lodge or château, and established a zoo on the site. The Emperor Matthias discovered — in the course of a day's hunting in 1619 — the beautiful spring that gave its name (schönen Brunnen) to the palace and supplied it with water un-

til the late 18th century. After the destruction of the château by the Turks, Johann Bernhard Fischer von Erlach designed a grand new building (on Leopold I's order, in 1692-93), intended to surpass by far the lavishness of Versailles, and to be situated on what is now the hill of the Gloriette (Gloriettehügel). A simpler edifice was practically finished in 1700, and the Emperor Josef I enjoyed agreeable stays there. His son, Karl VI, neglected the building plans; they were finished by Maria Theresa, thus giving Schönbrunn its present form. N. Pacassi, followed by Valmagini, completed the construction of the palace. The gardens were designed, in the French style, by Jean Trehet in 1705-06; but their present appearance is the result of work from 1753 to 1775 by Ferdinand

Schönbrunn Palace: the hall of mirrors.

Schönbrunn Palace: main hall.

von Hohenberg and Adrian van Steckhoven. With the Hofburg, Schönbrunn has been the favourite residence first of Roman-Germanic and then Austrian emperors, since the time of Maria Theresa. Altogether 1,441 rooms and halls lodged the court; of these, 390 were given over to living quarters and the scene of the court itself. 139 kitchens served almost 1,000 persons; and, with an area of 1.76 sq.km, Schönbrunn was for example four times larger than the Vatican.

Schönbrunn was the scene of dazzling receptions during the Congress of Vienna in 1814-15. Napoleon's only son, who became Duke of Reichstadt, lived and died here. The Emperor Franz Josef was born at Schönbrunn in 1830, and died here in 1916. In 1918 the Emperor Karl I abdicated his imperial crown here. The whole palace was very heavily damaged in the second World War: it was hit by 270 bombs. From 1945 to 1947 it was the headquarters of the occupying British troops. The extensive restoration works were completed in 1952; these luxurious salons are now the scene of diplomatic receptions.

The most outstanding features of the magnificent parkland at Schönbrunn, which covers an area of 197 hectares, are Neptune's Fountain, the Obelisk and the Roman Ruins. The flowery gardens stretch as far as

The Austrian-Hungarian monarchy's coat of arms.

Coach Museum.

UNO buildings.

The Danube Tower
(Donauturm). ▷

Danube Park.

Chess in Danube Park.

the summit of a hill surmounted by the Gloriette. This open colonnade, 19 metres high and 95 m long, was built by Ferdinand von Hohenberg and is flanked by trophies and Roman suits of armour. The hall in the middle, whouse large windows were formerly closed with glass, was often used for Court festivities. From the terrace, which is reached by means of a spiral staircase, the visitor can enjoy one of the most beautiful panoramas of Vienna.

The sumptuous accommodation in the interior of the château is decorated in the rococo style. The salons of Schönbrunn were for a long time the historic setting for the activities of the Viennese court.

The great hall merits special attention; splendid glass lamps hang from the ceiling, which is decorated with frescoes by Guglielmi. The formal court banquets were held in this hall, often with more than a hundred guests.

Other parts of the palace of artistic and historical interest include: the Emperor Franz Josef I's office, with portraits of the Empress Elisabeth in 1863 and of the Emperor Josef at 30 years old, both by Franz Russ; the Small Gallery, decorated by Albert Boller in 1761; and the Horses Room, with engravings on copper by Johann Georg von Hamilton. Also Napoleon's Room, where the French emperor lived in 1805 and 1809 when he had his headquarters at Schönbrunn; the Porcelain Room, the Gobelins Room, and the Red Hall.

The building on the east side of the château,

DAS RIESENRAD WURDE
1896-97 VON DEM ENGLISCHEN
ING. WALTER BASSET ERBAUT.
ES IST 64.75 m HOCH. SEIN
GEWICHT BETRAGT 430.05 t.
DIE ACHSENMITTE BEFINDET
SICH 34.2 m ÜBER DEM BODEN.
ES DREHT SICH MIT EINER
GESCHWINDIGKEIT VON 0.75 m
IN DER SEKUNDE. 1945 IST ES
INFOLGE KRIEGSEINWIRKUNG
AUSGEBRANNT. 1947 WURDE
ES WIEDERHERGESTELLT.

The "Prater"
Funfair.

The great
Ferris wheel.

previously occupied by Schönbrunn's winter riding school, now houses a museum of historic coaches, some sumptuous and others utilitarian, known as the "Coaches Palace." With 130 exhibits, this is the largest collection of coaches in the world.

The more important protagonists of history who have lived in the palace include — among others — the Emperor Josef I, the Empress Maria Theresa, Leopold II, his son Franz I and Emperor Ferdinand I. Particular mention should be made of the Emperor Franz Josef I and his wife Elisabeth, commonly known as Sissi. Franz Josef I was born at Schönbrunn on the 18th August 1830, lived and died here — on the 16th November 1916, in the midst of the world war. He worked for years here, until the end of a life that was marked by a tragic destiny. His wife was assassinated in 1898 and his son Rudolf, the crown prince, committed suicide in Mayerling Castle in 1889.

GRINZING AND THE OUTSKIRTS OF VIENNA

Grinzing is undoubtably the best-known district of Döbling. As early as 1114 it was mentioned, as "Grinzingan," in documents; today it is known the world over as Vienna's typical Heurigenort (district of young, home-grown wine). The wine drunk in Grinzing is very refreshing, but mischievous: it can easily have an inebriating effect, which is why the Viennese do not usually drink it without first eating copiously. Otto Stradal writes that "The Viennese always provide themselves with a Heurigenpackerl, or picnic, to alleviate the effect of the alcohol." Many of the typical taverns also serve Wiener Backhenderln (roast chicken in the Viennese style). An unashamedly jolly atmosphere reigns when the people of Vienna play Schrammeln. This form of music peculiar to Vienna — involving two violins, a guitar and an accordion, and named after the Schrammel brothers, successful

Grinzing: the Wine-growing Museum.

composers of music in Vienna — helps the Viennese to forget their day-to-day worries.

The village of Grinzing, lying between gardens and vineyards, still displays — with its historic buildings — the pleasant image of times past. One should visit the picturesque Old House in Himmelstrasse, the Hauermandl in Cobenzlgasse, the courtyard of the house at no. 9 Cobenzlgasse, and the attractive late Gothic parish church. A visit to this enchanting village on the outskirts of Vienna, thus, always leaves a pleasant memory, and those who have been so fortunate as to have been there look forward to returning to Grinzing as soon as they can, as the chorus of a Viennese song says. In the agreeable little museum of wine at Grinzing one can study the history of its production. There are other wine-growing villages around Vienna

Vineyards at Grinzing.

Heurigen (taverns). ▷

famous for their wine: Sievering, Nussdorf and Heiligenstadt. A wine-grower's house in Heiligenstadt became world-famous because, in 1807, Beethoven lived there and wrote his celebrated Pastoral Symphony. Although they now form part of the capital, these picturesque villages have not lost their rural charm.

EXCURSIONS FROM VIENNA

Hinterbrühl bei Mödling is one of the most interesting places in the environs of Vienna. It is 20 kilometres from the capital by road and includes the attraction of the Seegrotte ("lake grotto"), an impressive subterranean lake of 6,200 sq.m, considered to be the largest of its kind in Europe.

In 1848 there was a gypsum mine on this site and when, in 1912, a fissure opened, twenty million litres of water flooded the cavern. Twenty years later the abandoned mine became a tourist attraction as an underground lake. In 1944, during the second World War, the Heinkel firm took over the cave and converted it into an aeroplane factory. After the end of the war the Seegrotte was opened to the public again.

The impressive forests occupying an enormous area of the hills surrounding Vienna are another great attraction. On clear days a marvellous panorama of the Austrian capital city can be enjoyed from the heights of Leopoldsberg or Kahlenberg. These woodlands extending over the hills and mountains in the vicinity of Vienna were used as a military vantage-point by the Austrian army fighting the Turkish troops who tried in vain to take the city.

The Wachau area is a particularly enchanting place in the environs of Vienna, it is held to be the most beautiful part of the Danube valley. Schneeberg and Rax — two peaks 2,000 metres high — or Puszta, in Burgenland, are particularly charming places as regards landscape, as is also the zone of the Danube's banks, which can be admired by making a boat trip.

Traditional music.

Two characteristic aspects of Jugendstil.

THE MAGIC OF VIENNESE MUSIC

Vienna is the homeland not only of great music — the music associated with the names of Haydn, Mozart, Beethoven, Schubert, Brahms and Strauss — but also of popular music, the music of Schrammel. He composed the greater part of the songs and pieces which make up the repertory of the itinerant quartets whose performances enliven the atmosphere in taverns of suburbs such as Neustift am Walde, Dornbach, Salmannsdorf, Grinzing, Heiligenstadt, Sievering, Nussdorf and other wine-growers' villages situated in the environs of Vienna.

The gaiety of popular music converts the typical taverns into elated centres for the life of ordinary people. Wine and music create an alliance which makes the hours pass pleasantly. A couple of violinists, a guitarist and an accordion-player help to make spirits joyful when they play popular compositions.

VIENNA AND JUGENDSTIL

Jugendstil — "modern style" in England, *art nouveau* in France, or *Modernismo* in Spain — derives from the name of the Munich magazine *Jugend*. In German-speaking countries it designates the style that triumphed in the greater part of western Europe at the turn of the century; in Spain one should refer to the work of the brilliant architect Antoni Gaudí. In Vienna it represented a kind of resurrection of the baroque style — which had an illustrious tradition there — with Romantic additions, giving rise to an exuberantly decorative school with predominantly floral symbols and undulating forms.

In Vienna there survive many buildings and monuments representative of Jugendstil, especially the Underground exits in Karlsplatz and a house in Linke Wienzeile. Jugendstil's extension of the baroque style produced a creative synthesis.

Heiligenkreuz.

HEILIGENKREUZ MONASTERY

This fine Cistercian abbey stands in the southern Wienerwald. It was built around 1135 by Leopold III, Austria's patron saint. Heiligenkreuz — Holy Cross — monastery is situated in an extraordinarily beautiful landscape impregnated with a fascinating atmosphere of romantic silence.

The interior of the church is an interesting specimen of Cistercian architecture; the monastery's cloister is also of great interest. The 18th-century Trinity Column stands opposite the façade of the church.

On the right of the entrance to the village of Heiligenkreuz there is a little cemetery with, on the left of its entrance, the tomb of Baroness Maria Vetsera who — with the Crown Prince Rudolf — committed suicide at Mayerling on the 30th January 1889.

Near the monastery are the Liechtenstein ruins, all that remains of a 12th-century castle. It suffered terrible devastations over the years, the worst being the ravages of the Turks in 1683. It has recently been rebuilt in accordance with its original appearance. This castle was the cradle of the dynasty that still reigns in Liechtenstein.

Perchtoldsdorf is a picturesque village also situated in this area to the south of Vienna, it retains a beautiful Gothic church and a fortified tower in the late Gothic style.

Another important monument not far from Heiligenkreuz is the Augustinian monastery, one of the oldest in Austria, with estimable works of art in its museum.

Mayerling church.

The hunting lodge at Mayerling.

The Woods of Vienna (Wienerwald).

Sunset over the woods and city of Vienna.

MAYERLING CASTLE

Separated from the Cistercian monastery of Heiligenkreuz by a beautiful forested valley, in the midst of the densest, most romantic woodlands imaginable, stands the historic castle of Mayerling. In 1889 the Archduke Rudolf (the Emperor Franz Josef I's only son and, therefore, heir to the throne of the Austro-Hungarian Empire) and his lover, the young Baroness Maria Vetsera, committed suicide in the hunting lodge here. These romantic, mysterious deaths shook late 19th-century Europe. The double suicide had far-reaching political consequences since with it the sovereign of one of the empires most vital to the stability of Europe at that time, Franz Josef I, was left without a direct successor to his throne.

After the sensational double suicide Mayerling Castle was converted, by decision of the Emperor Franz Josef, into a Carmelite convent.

It is now one of the most popular tourist sites in the environs of Vienna. The surroundings are really extremely beautiful, and in perfect harmony with the tragic atmosphere left by the suicide of the archduke and his lover. Historians, novelists and film-makers have on many occasions given their attention to Mayerling, attempting — with greater or lesser degrees of success and realism — to unravel the mystery that the Archduke Rudolf took with him to his grave.

Contents

The printing of this book was completed
in the workshops of FISA - Industrias
Gráficas, Palaudarias, 26 - Barcelona
(Spain)